The Central Pacific Railroad

CORNERSTONES OF FREEDOM

SECOND SERIES

Clark J. Evans

Children's Press®
A Division of Scholastic Inc.
New York • Toronto • London • Auckland • Sydney
Mexico City • New Delhi • Hong Kong
Danbury, Connecticut

Photographs ©, 2003: Art Resource, NY: 3, 44 (Museum of the City of New York/Scala), 28 (National Portrait Gallery, Smithsonian Institution); Brown Brothers: 10 left, 11 top right, 16, 38; California State Railroad Museum Library, Sacramento, CA: cover top; Corbis Images: 35 (James L. Amos), 17, 45 bottom (Bettmann), 4 (J.C.H. Grabill), 45 top right (Joseph Sohm/ChromoSohm Inc.), 5, 7, 13; Hulton|Archive/Getty Images: 29, 32; Photo Researchers, NY: 37 (Deseret News), 23, 24, 25, 26, 34 (Alfred A. Hart Photo), 39 bottom, 39 top (Southern Pacific Photo), 40, 41; Stock Montage, Inc.: cover bottom, 36; Superstock, Inc.: 11 bottom, 45 top left (The Huntington Library, Art Collections, and Botanical Gardens,San Marino, California); The Image Works/Jeff Greenberg: 19; Union Pacific Historical Collection: 8, 10 right, 11 top left, 21, 22, 30, 31.

Library of Congress Cataloging-in-Publication Data

Evans, Clark J.

  The Central Pacific Railroad / Clark J. Evans.

    p. cm.— (Cornerstones of freedom)

  Summary: Discusses the 1860s construction of the Central Pacific Railroad, or Transcontinental Railroad, and the financial backers and workers involved in this project that reduced coast-to-coast travel from over one hundred days to six.

Includes bibliographical references and index.

  ISBN 0-516-22677-0

  1. Central Pacific Railroad Company—History—Juvenile literature.
2. Railroads—United States—History—19th century—Juvenile literature. [1. Central Pacific Railroad Company. 2. Railroads—History.]
I. Title. II. Series.

  TF25.C4 E93 2003

  385'.0973—dc21

                              2002009027

1 2 3 4 5 6 7 8 9 10 R 12 11 10 09 08 07 06 05 04 03

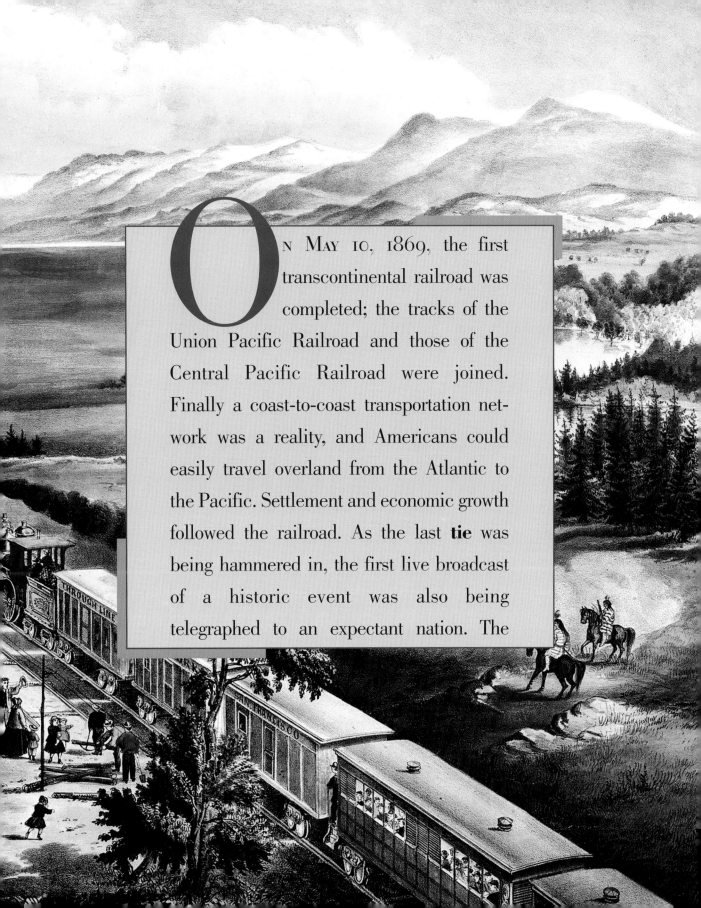

ON MAY 10, 1869, the first transcontinental railroad was completed; the tracks of the Union Pacific Railroad and those of the Central Pacific Railroad were joined. Finally a coast-to-coast transportation network was a reality, and Americans could easily travel overland from the Atlantic to the Pacific. Settlement and economic growth followed the railroad. As the last **tie** was being hammered in, the first live broadcast of a historic event was also being telegraphed to an expectant nation. The

In the early 19th century, before the railroad was built, wagon trains were the most common way for settlers to travel west.

simple word "Done" was transmitted across the continent and touched off a national celebration the likes of which had never before been seen in the United States. In New York, a one-hundred-cannon salute was fired, Wall Street shut down, and special prayers were offered up in Trinity Church. Chicagoans spontaneously started a parade that eventually grew to 7 miles (11.3 kilometers) in length. Philadelphians rang the Liberty Bell. People across the nation rang church bells, clanged fire engines, boomed cannons, and lit bonfires. The country rejoiced.

MANIFEST DESTINY

For almost two centuries American settlers had advanced slowly westward. The trip across the country west of the Mississippi River was very dangerous. Travelers had to deal with attacks by Native Americans, and the risk of contracting **cholera** or other fatal diseases was great. Traveling was risky because of the lawlessness that existed in the West at that time. In addition to land routes, there were other ways to reach California and the West Coast. One was to travel by ship down the East Coast of the United States and then **portage** across the Central

★ ★ ★ ★

American country of Panama, which is only 50 miles (80.5 km) wide at one point, then sail northwest to California or other places on the West Coast. Not long before the transcontinental railroad project was started, a railroad was built to cross the **Isthmus of Panama.** This cut travel time, but the danger of contracting a disease such as malaria or yellow fever was still great. Another way to reach California was to sail around the tip of South America, known as Cape Horn, a 17,000-mile (27,360-km) trip.

Many Americans in the nineteenth century believed that it might take another two centuries to settle the huge territory between the two coasts. But it did not matter how long it took; the general belief was that United States expansion across the continent was **divinely ordained.** People believed that it was inevitable that one day the United States—its democracy, its culture, and its population—would extend from the Atlantic Ocean to the Pacific Ocean. God, they thought, had ordained that this was America's Manifest Destiny, meaning it was America's clear and unmistakable mission to control the entire continent. The railroad would provide the means to carry out this mission.

SLAVERY, POLITICS, AND THE RAILROAD

In the middle of the nineteenth century, Congress was debating the issue of which of the new territories—including the Utah territory and what would become the New Mexico territory—would allow the institution of slavery. Which

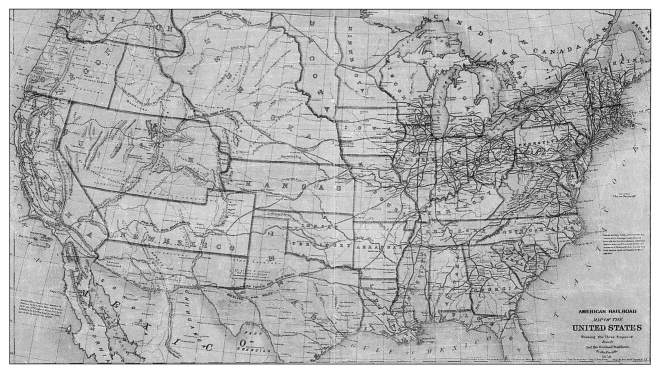

This railroad map, drawn in 1859, shows the existing rail lines in the United States and its western territories as well as several different proposed routes for the transcontinental railroad.

territories would be admitted to the United States as free states and which as slave states was a question on everyone's mind. Despite a Congressional **stalemate** over the future of slavery in these newly acquired lands, California, the thirty-first state, entered the Union as a free state in 1850. The many newcomers who had migrated to California from the East Coast in search of the gold found there in 1849 had been required to either sail around the tip of South America, cross the jungles in Panama, or tramp across the entire continent to settle there. Californians wanted an easier way to be connected to the rest of the states: they wanted a railroad.

Theodore Judah (1826-1863) had engineered numerous railroad construction projects by the time he was twenty-eight.

JEFFERSON DAVIS AND THE CONFEDERACY

By the time the Central Pacific Railroad began

construction, the Civil War had begun, and Jefferson

Davis had been elected president of the Confederacy.

The idea of a transcontinental railroad was supported by many in the U.S. Congress. The problem was deciding what route the railroad should take. If it took a northern path, proslavery Congressmen were afraid that free states would develop along the route. Meanwhile, antislavery Congressmen were concerned that if the railroad started in a Southern state, slavery would follow in its path. Neither side wanted the balance of power to shift in favor of the other side. The slavery issue stood in the way of any concrete plans for a transcontinental railroad.

PLANNING THE ROUTE

Even with debate over the route, Congress realized that it would be necessary to have a better means of transportation to connect the nation's two coasts. In 1853, Congress authorized Secretary of War Jefferson Davis to carry out surveys to find out whether a transcontinental railroad was practical or even possible.

In 1853, army engineers, under the direction of Davis, set out to find the best route to the Pacific. The surveys showed that four possible routes could be followed. Davis, being a Southerner, favored the southern route. But the route that was finally used was surveyed by Theodore H. Judah, an engineer who had given up a high-paying position in 1854 to go to California to build the Sacramento Valley Railroad, the first railroad to be built on the Pacific Coast. Judah had been educated at the Troy Engineering School. He had been responsible for surveying and building the Niagara Gorge Railroad from Niagara Falls to Lewiston, New York, and served as a designing engineer on the Erie Canal and on the Rochester and Niagara Falls Railroad.

Judah, whose dream was to build a Pacific railroad to connect California with the rest of the United States, believed that if he could find a pass through the Sierra Nevada range that would make construction cheaper and more practical, the next U.S. president would approve construction plans. The only problem was that Judah, working alone, did not have the money to conduct a survey. He turned to friends he had made in Northern California, who helped raise the money for the expedition and provided men to help him.

What Judah found was a pass, 128 miles (206 km) east of Sacramento, through which the Sierra Nevada range could be crossed. The pass was not very steep and would be suitable for a railroad. He estimated the cost to cross there would save $150,000 a mile, plus 184 miles (296.1 km) in distance, over any of the routes the government engineers had recommended. The total savings would come to more than $13,500,000.

Judah returned to California and journeyed to San Francisco to try to convince wealthy businessmen to finance the

THE BEAUTY OF THE MOUNTAINS

Judah's wife, Anna, went along with the surveying party. While her husband and the men were working, she fished to provide food for their meals. When she thought she had enough fish to prepare dinner, she would draw the majestic Sierra Nevada. Two of her drawings later appeared on the stock certificates of the Central Pacific Railroad, some were used in her husband's presentations, and others were used to show the rest of the country the beauty of the California mountains.

The Big Four—From left to right: Leland Stanford (1824-1893), Charles Crocker (1822-1888), Mark Hopkins (1821-1900), and Collis P. Huntington (1813-1878)—were all easterners who had come to California to make their fortunes.

project, but they found the idea of completing a project on that scale and making it profitable unlikely and amusing, and they turned him away. But Judah did not give up. Returning to Sacramento, he persuaded some wealthy local merchants, Leland Stanford, Charles Crocker, Mark Hopkins, and Collis P. Huntington—later known as the Big Four—to invest in a railroad that would go from Nevada to California.

The Big Four's decision to build the railroad was based on their sense of a good opportunity, in addition to their

interest in increasing their personal wealth. Abraham Lincoln had been elected sixteenth president on November 6, 1860 and a civil war seemed unavoidable as Southern states began to secede from the Union. All of the Big Four were supporters of Lincoln and the Union cause. A railroad running east from California would keep the state from being isolated from the rest of the Union. Plus a railroad line running into Nevada would be very profitable, considering the location of the Comstock and Virginia City mines in western Nevada. With these facts in mind, on June 28, 1861, the Big Four incorporated the

Before becoming president of the United States, Abraham Lincoln had many railroads as clients while he was a lawyer in Springfield, Illinois.

11

Central Pacific Railroad Company of California. That same summer Stanford campaigned for the governorship of the state, winning election in September to a two-year term.

THE FIRST RAILROAD ACT

In October 1861, Judah was sent to Washington, D.C., by the Central Pacific Railroad Company of California to **lobby** the United States government for **appropriations** of land and **bonds**. Congress had many questions about the way the railroad would be built. Why should the railroad be built through solid mountains at a rate of only 4 feet (1.2 meters) a day? The answer was that this was the only way to get across the Sierra Nevada without bypassing the mountains. The route through the Sierra Nevada range was the one route that would cut travel time to cross the United States down to six days by railroad. Also, going through the mountains was the only way to build the railroad across the country. Building the railroad across the Northern states would take longer, and it would be too cold for workers to keep going through the coldest months of the year. Also, any Southern route was out of the question because the Civil War had already begun, and the Union-based railroads would not be able to cross the Confederate South, which extended as far west as Texas and Oklahoma and as far north as parts of Missouri. The middle route over the Sierra Nevada range was the best possible way.

Judah finally managed to convince Congress to pass the first Pacific Railway Act, which President Lincoln signed on

The rugged Sierra Nevada mountain range was the greatest barrier to the eastern construction of the railroad.

July 1, 1862, after years of debate on the best route. Thus began one of the greatest adventures in American history.

Under the terms of the Railroad Act, the Central Pacific was authorized to build from California toward the east from Sacramento through the Sierra Nevada mountain range. The Act also **chartered** a new company, the Union Pacific Railroad, to build west from the 100th meridian (near Omaha,

Nebraska) across the Great Plains into Nevada or until it met the Central Pacific line. Together they were authorized to construct a railroad and telegraph line that would connect the continent. The U.S. government granted the railroads right-of-way, the legal right to pass through federally owned land. They received money, a construction **subsidy** in the form of United States bonds, from the U.S. government. The funds were paid out at different rates for building the route. The rate was $16,000 a mile to build on level land east of the Rocky Mountains. In the mountainous areas the railroad would receive $48,000 per mile, and for construction in the rolling hills between the mountains the rate was $32,000. This was actually a loan. The bonds were to be repaid over thirty years at an interest rate of 6 percent. The government set a deadline of twelve years for the railroad to finish construction. As incentive, the companies were given 20 miles (32.2 km) of land on each side of the tracks through open spaces. The government promised additional money to each of the railroads, the amount depending on how much track was laid. This resulted in strong competition between the two lines.

CONSTRUCTION BEGINS

The groundbreaking ceremony, marking the official start of construction on the Central Pacific Railroad, was held on January 1, 1863. Surrounded by members of the legislature and state and city officials, California governor Stanford stood at the foot of K Street in Sacramento and shoveled some sand into a mud hole. Then Governor Stanford said, "We may now look forward with confidence to the day, not far distant, when the Pacific Coast will be bound to the Atlantic Coast by iron bonds that shall consolidate and strengthen the ties of nationality, and advance with giant strides the prosperity of the state and country. . . ." The crowd of onlookers found the thought of a bunch of local businessmen attempting to build a railroad across the continent quite strange. The Union Pacific broke ground at the Missouri River bluffs near Omaha, Nebraska, on December 2, 1863.

During the early months of 1863, Theodore Judah began work on making the final plans for the portion of the route that would cross the mountains. In the summer of 1863, he hired a twenty-five-year-old engineer, Lewis Clement, to assist him. Clement would later be named acting chief engineer. Judah developed so much faith in Clement that he sent Clement out alone to conduct a survey that involved studying the mountains and their features and then putting together a detailed map from the information he had gathered.

FATHER OF THE RAILROAD

Theodore Judah, the man who has been called the father of the transcontinental railroad, sadly did not live to see it completed. In 1863, he had a dispute with the Big Four and went to New York to raise money to buy them out. He took the route across Panama, caught yellow fever—a tropical disease spread by mosquitoes—on the trip, and died a few days after arriving in New York.

Then the two men worked together day and night until they decided on the best route over the mountains. The two worked so well together that Judah put Clement in charge of building the most difficult stretch of the railroad, the section that crossed over the summit of the Sierra Nevada range, running from Colfax to Truckee, California.

THE CHINESE AND THE RAILROAD

The first 23 miles (37 km) were easy to set in place. But the railroad company soon ran into problems. Workers were not as easy to come by as they had supposed. Manpower was hard to come by in many of the regions where the railroad was built. Also, many men would start working for the railroad and ride with their crews to the work site by train. The route of the railroad passed through mining regions, and whenever news of a new strike reached the hired men, many

Gold miners pose for the camera. The discovery of gold in California in 1849 attracted thousands of newcomers to the state.

would desert their railroad jobs and head off for the mines. Others accepted employment with the railroad just to get a ride to search for gold on their own.

Crocker, the member of the Big Four who had taken over the responsibility of supervising the work in the field, wanted to try out Chinese laborers because California's Foreign Miners Tax of 1850, a twenty-dollar-per-month fee, made it almost impossible for the Chinese workers to mine or prospect for gold. Many Chinese men were coming to the

Chinese workers hired to build the railroad pitched tents along the work site.

United States because China was torn by war and foreign invasion, and they had no money, jobs, or land.

In January 1865, Crocker hired Chinese workers at a salary of about twenty-eight dollars per month, even though he wasn't sure they could handle the hard work. At that time there was a great deal of prejudice against the Chinese workers in California, and they were immediately segregated by the crews of white workers. To Crocker's surprise, they worked harder than any of his other men. Although most were smaller than the Americans, they did not take breaks to smoke and talk. They would stop only to drink a cup of tea, and then they would go right back to work. Another advantage of employing Chinese workers was that they worked for less money than did their white counterparts. And they used only their own cooks and kitchens, asking the railroad for the cost of food alone. In fact, the Chinese laborers did their jobs so well that the Central Pacific eventually hired ten thousand more Chinese men.

Work on the railroad required an enormous amount of blasting through rock. Because gunpowder had been invented in China, many of the Chinese were experts at using it. They would hang over the sides of a cliff in baskets, chiseling at the granite, and planting explosives in small holes bored in the rock. Once the charges were in place, other workers had to haul the men back up as quickly as possible. Approximately one out of every ten Chinese workers died as a result of accidents or the cold.

BRINGING THE SUPPLIES TO THE FRONT

Getting the necessary supplies to the railroad construction site when they were needed was a highly complicated matter. Because there were not many factories outside the East, it took a long time to get necessary supplies to the railroad construction site in California. Everything had to be ordered months in advance. In order to lay each mile of track, 352 rails, 2,500 ties, 14,000 nuts and bolts, and 28,160 spikes had to be imported. In addition, the locomotives,

Stanford University in Palo Alto, California, which opened its doors on October 1, 1891, was founded by Leland Stanford and his wife, Jane, in memory of their only child, Leland, Jr.

THE GOVERNOR STANFORD

The first steam engine to be used by the railroad was shipped from Boston, Massachusetts, on May 16, 1863, and traveled around the tip of South America on the ship *Herald of the Morning*. The engine arrived in San Francisco, California, on September 20, 1863. The steam engine was then transferred to a river schooner named the *Artful Dodger*, which arrived in Sacramento, California, on October 5, 1863. The railroad threw a big party and named the steam engine the *Governor Stanford* after Leland Stanford. The first steam engine cost $13,688 to build.

switch mechanisms, and foundry tools had to be brought in. Shovels, axes, quarry tools, crowbars, wheelbarrows, dump carts, horse-drawn scrapers, and blasting powder could not be purchased on the West Coast. Once ordered, goods had to be shipped in the same way people traveled westward: by wagon or by ship. Because the land west of the Mississippi River was made up mostly of deserts, prairies, and mountains, efficiently shipping goods across land would have been almost impossible. Ship was the only practical and economical means of transportation, but using ships meant sailing 17,000 miles (27,360 km) around Cape Horn. Only brick, stone, and wood for cross ties, bridges, and structures were available from West Coast sources. To make things even more complicated, the construction site of the railroad was a moving target, advancing sometimes faster, sometimes slower, from west to east.

LAYING THE TRACK

Laying track was done in the same way by both railroad companies. The men were divided up into specialized crews, which operated in much the same way as an assembly line does today. The front of the line and the back of the line were separated by 100 to 200 miles (160 to 320 km). In that way work could continuously progress. No one had to wait while the crew in front finished their portion of the work. The first crew sent out conducted a preliminary survey and was followed by another group who made a location survey. Next came the graders, the men who made the ground flat enough for the track to be laid. They would grade 100 miles (160 km) at a time, except in the mountains, where they would work as much as 200 to 300 miles (320 to 480 km) ahead of the crew following, as this took so much longer. Then the bridge, **trestle**, and **culvert** crews followed, working 5 to 20 miles (8 to 32 km) ahead of the track layers. As the track layers came along, they would grab rails out of horse-drawn carts. At the end of the line were the men who hammered in the spikes. Every 100 to 200 miles (160 to 320 km), the base camp would move up.

WORK PROGRESSES

From Sacramento, California, the railroad reached Roseville, California, in February 1864. From Roseville, the tracks headed to Rocklin, California, which became a

Originally named Junction, the Roseville, California, railroad station linked the towns Lincoln and Folsom.

major railroad service center. While the route to Newcastle, California, was being built, the railroad ran out of money, and construction could not continue.

To provide more funds, Congress passed the Pacific Railway Act of 1864. This act allowed the railroad companies to issue their own bonds. It also doubled the land grants, giving the railroad companies another way to raise money. In April 1865, the Central Pacific Railroad began laying track again and reached Auburn, California, in May 1865. Only 40 miles (64 km) had been completed then. In September 1865 the railroad reached Colfax, California, which would become a major supply center. As it grew,

Colfax, California, was named for Schuyler Colfax, the speaker of the House of Representatives from 1863 to 1869. It started as a central transportation, communications, and gathering place for the Central Pacific.

Tunneling through the Sierra Nevada was the greatest challenge faced by the Central Pacific's engineers and laborers.

Colfax served as a junction for stagecoach lines until the railroad was completed. Many new small towns such as Iowa Hill, Gold Run, and Emigrant Gap were born because of the building of the railroad. The easy part of the route was now complete.

To make it through the Sierra Nevada range, workers had to construct fifteen tunnels between Sacramento, California, and Promontory Summit, Utah. In addition, they had to

Snow sheds like this one prevented too much snow from accumulating on the tracks of the railway.

make high trestles, deep fills, and incredible rock cuts. They had to build thirty-seven snow sheds to keep the snow off the tracks. Snow sheds were long, open-ended sheds made of heavy timber to protect a section of track from deep snow and avalanches. The snow sheds were quite a sight. They were built for 40 miles (64 km) and ranged from 50 to 200 feet (15.2 to 61 m) long. Most of the tunnels the trains ran through had curves in them, which were very hard to build at that time. The rock that was blasted off the sides of the mountains and from the tunnels was used to fill in any uneven areas. The average forward movement for building the tunnels through the granite rock was only about 3 feet (.91 m) a day.

THE CHINESE WALL

Between the seventh and eighth tunnel the workers built what was called the "Chinese Wall." It was a wall built 75 feet (22.9 m) high to hold a path for the train to go over. The cliffs were so steep that it was almost 1,200 feet (365 m) straight down to the American River. Many times the Chinese workers had to drive stakes into the sides of the mountains to hook ropes to so they could have something to hold on to.

Early travelers take a moment to look down from the "Chinese Wall" onto the American River.

★ ★ ★ ★

A train passes through Emigrant, near where the Donner Party was trapped and perished in the winter of 1846.

TOP OF THE MOUNTAIN/ON TO THE EAST

The Central Pacific reached Cisco, California, only 94 miles (151.3 km) from Sacramento, on November 9, 1866. It was here that the Chinese workers blasted tunnel six. For this purpose, they built the first **nitroglycerin** factory, near Donner Lake. In November and December of 1866, there were many snowstorms, but not enough to stop the work on the tunnels. The rough, rocky sides of Donner Peak soon became smooth from all the snow. Donner Peak, along with Donner Lake and Donner Pass, was named after the Donner party, a group of pioneers who died when they got caught in an early storm while trying to cross the mountains there.

Tunnel six, which came to be called the Summit Tunnel, took two years to build. It was 1,659 feet (505.7 m) long and was built from three openings at the same time. It was built not only from each end toward the center but also from the top of the mountain by means of an 8-foot-by-12-foot (2.4-m-by-3.7-m) shaft that went 73 feet (22 m) down to what would be the middle of the tunnel. Once the railroad workers reached rock that was to be the bottom of the shaft, they began to dig outward in two directions in order to meet up with the workers digging from the outer ends of the tunnel. By digging in this way, more men could work on the tunnel at the same time. When the railroad line was completed, the shaft would also serve to release the smoke from the train engines. It took eighty-five days just to construct the shaft. The first train

HOW DID THE WAGONS CROSS?

It was hard to get wagons, goods, and people down off the mountains in places where the wagon trains could not find a level area to travel. First, stakes were driven into the side of the mountain and the wagons were lowered by rope. Next, horses would be lowered by rope to a place where it was not too steep to travel. People would be lowered last.

Captain John C. Fremont was the first to see the Washoe Native Americans in 1844.

28

ran through the Summit Tunnel on November 30, 1867.

The path to tunnels eight and nine could not be used because of the ice and snow. The men were able to continue tunnel digging during bad winter weather because they blocked the tunnel openings with wood so the tunnels could act as shelter. There were forty-four storms in the area that winter, ranging from a short snow **squall** to a two-week-long gale. The heaviest storm lasted from February 18 to February 22, 1867, during which 6 feet (1.8 m) of snow fell. March 2, 1867, saw the end of a thirteen-day storm.

During all the time that was spent digging the tunnels, there were also workers to the east, building the section of the railroad running east and west of Truckee, near the California-Nevada border. Everything the men needed was taken by wagons from the western end of the tunnels, 40 miles (64 km) around the mountains, to the work site. On the level land they were able to lay a mile of track a day. The tracks reached Truckee in April 1868.

The Washoe, a tribe of Native Americans, lived in this area. The railroad was destroying the Washoe's hunting grounds, so the tribe formed small bands and destroyed or took supplies from some of the trains. The Central Pacific Railroad workers could not fight back because they had no guns. The owners of the

Summit Tunnel at Donner Pass was used for 130 years by the Central Pacific Railroad.

The Central Pacific reached Nevada in 1868. At the time, the entire non-Native American population of the state was less than 40,000.

railroad company decided to give the Washoe food, metal tools, liquor, and free passage to ride the trains so they wouldn't have any more trouble. For many years afterward, the Washoe were able to ride free on the Central Pacific freight trains.

Building was a lot easier once the workers had the mountains behind them. One of the first towns beyond the mountains, Verdi, Nevada, was a big lumber town that sold a lot of wood to the railroad. Verdi also became a major station of the

Central Pacific line. The town soon earned a place in history when the first train robbery of the Old West took place there on November 5, 1870.

The railroad followed the Truckee River for 13 miles (21 km) and in June 1868 reached the town of Lake's Crossing, just inside the Nevada border. The town was renamed Reno and became a major trading center. In Reno the railroad sold parcels of land, 60 feet by 60 feet (18.3 m by 18.3 m), for twelve hundred dollars each. The land was valuable

Express companies such as Wells Fargo, whose Reno station is seen in this photograph, provided the main form of overland transportation in the West before the railroad.

HOW RENO GOT ITS NAME

Crocker decided to rename the town of Lake's Crossing to honor all of the famous officers from both the North and the South who were killed in battle during the Civil War. Their names were placed in a hat. The one that was selected was that of General Jesse Reno, and so the town came to be called Reno.

General Jesse Reno (1823-1862) died at the Battle of South Mountain during the Civil War.

because of its proximity to silver mines in Virginia City. Reno's location and the presence of the railroad made it an excellent spot for a distribution center. In 1868 the town east of Reno—Wadsworth, Nevada—became a major repair site for the railroad.

When the Union Pacific reached the Wasatch Mountains in the winter of 1868–1869, the company made the decision to go north of Salt Lake City, Utah, to avoid the salt flats west of the lake. Brigham Young was the head of the Mormon Church, which had settled Utah in 1848. Young was very upset about the Union Pacific's decision and said he would not send the Mormon workers he had promised. But when the Central Pacific also decided to go north, he made up his mind to build his own railroad to connect with the Union Pacific.

BRIGHAM YOUNG'S RAILROAD

Because the Union Pacific could not pay its total bill to the Mormons, who had supplied a large number of workers for the building effort in Utah, they were forced to give Brigham Young $600,000 worth of stock in the railroad. This was how Young was able to finance his own railroad.

Because both sides were paid by the amount of track they laid and the place where the two railroads would meet had never been firmly established, both sides kept building, eventually overlapping 80 miles (129 km). This overlap of track was never used and cost one million dollars to build. Congress finally met and decided that the Central Pacific and Union Pacific would meet at Promontory Summit, Utah. Now the race to the Summit began.

The Union Pacific Railroad was built from Omaha, Nebraska, to Promontory Summit, a distance of 992 miles (1,596 km). The Union Pacific built only four tunnels over the entire route. The combined length of all tunnels for the Central Pacific Railroad was 6,213 feet (1,894 m). The combined length of the Union Pacific tunnels was only 1,792 feet (546 m).

As the two railroads came within 23 miles (37 km) of meeting each other, the Union Pacific track crew laid 8 miles (12.9 km) of track in one day. Charles Crocker of the Central Pacific Railroad then bet Thomas Durant, the head foreman of the Union Pacific Railroad, ten thousand dollars that his workers could lay more than 10 miles (16.1 km) of track in one day. Crocker's men worked from sunrise to sunset on April 28, 1869, with five thousand men. They used 25,800 ties, 3,520 rails, and 28,160 spikes. On this one day the Central Pacific workers laid 10 miles (16.1 km) of track in twelve hours.

Chinese laborers clear a path for the Central Pacific Railroad

And at the end of the day, they were only 4 miles (6.4 km) from their final destination, the top of Promontory Summit. James H. Strobridge of the Central Pacific Railroad paid his men four days' wages for that single day of work. Durant never paid on the bet, and afterward, Crocker and Durant were no longer friends and did not speak much to each other.

THE FINISH LINE

On the morning of May 9, 1869, there was one length of rail separating the Union Pacific and Central Pacific lines. Governor Stanford had arrived at Promontory Summit on May 7.

They now awaited the arrival of Thomas Durant, the head foreman of the Union Pacific, whose train had been delayed en route. There were two golden spikes aboard Governor Stanford's train. One had been provided by the *San Francisco News Letter*; the other was made by one of the Central Pacific's largest supply contractors and had the names of all the Central Pacific directors engraved on it. Also aboard was a spike made of silver, gold, and iron, which had been provided by the governor of Arizona, and a silver spike, which had been sent from Virginia City, Nevada. The

THE GOLDEN SPIKE

On board the governor's special train were the last spikes to be used. The famous spike made of gold was among them. It was 6 inches (15.2 centimeters) long and weighed 18 ounces (0.51 kilograms). A gold nugget was attached to its point. This nugget was later used to make rings for President Ulysses S. Grant, Secretary of State William Seward, Governor Stanford, and others. It was removed shortly before the spike was driven.

35

The Central Pacific Railroad's "Jupiter" engine (left) meets the Union Pacific's "Engine 119" (right) at Promontory Summit, Utah, on May 10, 1869.

last tie to be used was made by the contractor who had supplied most of the Central Pacific's ties. It was made of waxed and hand-polished laurelwood. A silver-plated hammer was provided by the Union Pacific to gently drive the last spike into place. Four holes had already been drilled in the laurel tie so that the precious spikes would have to be tapped only once.

Finally, on the morning of May 10, the two trains from the East arrived. The ceremony began at noon. Only about six hundred people gathered to watch the monumental event. But people across the country eagerly awaited the telegraph message that would bring word that transcontinental travel by rail would now be a reality.

The ceremonial laurel tie was put in place. A group of Chinese workers carried out one rail, and a group of Irish workers carried the other. Durant of the Union Pacific placed the Arizona and Nevada spikes in the tie, then Stanford inserted the golden spikes. The silver-plated hammer was given to Durant and then to Stanford to gently tap in the spikes. The spikes, the laurel tie, and the silver-plated hammer were immediately removed and were replaced by an ordinary tie, three iron spikes, and a regular hammer.

The fourth iron spike and the hammer were wired to the transcontinental telegraph, so that when the hammer hit the spike the electrical circuit would be completed and the country would hear the telegraph click and know the

A crowd gathers around as the golden spike is about to be driven into the ground.

transcontinental railroad had become a reality. The telegraph operator then tapped out the message, "Done."

The two locomotives were driven toward each other until they touched. Then, the Central Pacific's locomotive backed up to allow the Union Pacific's engine to cross. Next, the Union Pacific let the Central Pacific cross. The laurel tie was cut up and the pieces given out to those selected to receive souvenirs.

This newspaper ran a front-page story about the completion of the transcontinental railroad.

A NATION UNITED

Across the United States, celebrations erupted. In San Francisco, the celebration expressed that city's boundless joy and lasted for three days. Around the country and around the world, train whistles blew, flags were flown from tall buildings, one-hundred-gun salutes were fired, and bonfires and fireworks lit up the night sky.

Manifest Destiny was now a reality. The spike that joined the Union Pacific and Central Pacific also united the East and the West and made the country whole—a continental nation.

In its first three months of operation, the Central Pacific Railroad earned a whopping $1,703,000. It reduced the length of the trip across the country from 149 days to just 6. The price of shipping goods to the West Coast dropped drastically. Consequently, more and more people were able to

Special smoking (above) and dining
cars (lower right) allowed railroad
passengers to travel in style.

travel to and settle the West. The country became truly one nation from coast to coast.

On the same land that many pioneers had died trying to cross just a few years earlier, towns and cities sprang up. Before long, seven transcontinental railroads had been constructed. The golden age of the railroad reached its peak just before the beginning of World War I.

THE RAILROAD AND TIME ZONES IN THE UNITED STATES

Today there are four different time zones in the continental United States. But it wasn't always that way. At the time the transcontinental railroad was completed, clocks everywhere were set according to the position of the sun. So it might have been 9:00 A.M. in one town and 9:05 A.M. in a town just 75 miles (121 km) away. Before high-speed railroads traveled across the country in six days, this was not much of a problem. But the need to avoid accidents and keep to a railroad schedule led to the adoption of standardized time zones. So today 9:00 A.M. in New York City is also 9:00 A.M. in Columbus, Ohio, 600 miles (966 km) away. And people in New York at 9:00 A.M. know that it is 6:00 A.M. everywhere in California.

* * * *

But there were also negative consequences. The railroad spelled the end of the magnificent wild buffalo herds. Men shot them from trains for sport and left them to rot. The Native American tribes, deprived of their land and their sources of food, were eventually conquered and placed on reservations.

Considering the small population and lack of wealth that existed in the country at the time the building of the railroad was undertaken, the primitive tools that the builders had to use, the state of technology at the time, the distance of the supplies from the work site, and the vast, harsh land the tracks had to cross, the transcontinental railroad is remembered as one of the greatest building achievements ever undertaken and successfully completed. The effect of this accomplishment on the course of United States history was **unprecedented** and may never be equaled.

A Central Pacific Railroad train makes its way through the Nevada Palisades.

Glossary

appropriations—money or other things of value set aside for a special purpose

bonds—certificates, or pieces of paper, that are sold with the promise of paying back the money, with interest, on a certain date

chartered—established by a government giving rights to a business, person, or institution

cholera—a severe intestinal disease caused by bacteria

culvert—a pipe used to divert, or turn, water from a path, in this case so the train can pass

divinely ordained—ordered or directed by God

Isthmus of Panama—a narrow strip of land with water on each side connecting North and South America

lobby—to try to persuade a public official to do something

Manifest Destiny—the belief that the United States had a duty to expand throughout the North American continent

nitroglycerin—an explosive used in dynamite

portage—to move boats or goods over land from one
      body of water to another

squall—a sudden violent wind accompanied by rain
      or snow

stalemate—a situation in which neither of two opposing
      sides can win (taken from a term used in the
      game of chess)

subsidy—money given by the government to help a
      person or company accomplish something

tie—the part of a railroad track that holds the two
      parallel rails in place, consisting of a long, thick
      piece of wood

trestle—a structure that is built to carry a train over
      a depression, or low spot, in the land

unprecedented—unlike anything that has happened before

Timeline: The Central

1850	1853	1854	1861
California is admitted to the Union under the Compromise of 1850 as the thirty-first state.	Congress authorizes Secretary of War Jefferson Davis to conduct official surveys for the proposed construction of a trans-continental railroad.	Theodore Judah surveys the route that is actually used when construction of the Central Pacific Railroad is begun.	The so-called Big Four incorporate the Central Pacific Railroad Company of California.

Pacific Railroad

1862

Congress passes the first Pacific Railway Act, which President Lincoln signs on July 1.

1863

The Central Pacific breaks ground in Sacramento, California on January 1; the Union Pacific breaks ground in Omaha, Nebraska, in December.

1865

The first group of what would grow to be more than ten thousand Chinese workers is hired.

1866–1868

Fifteen tunnels and thirty-seven snow sheds are constructed for the railroad to cross the Sierra Nevada range.

1868

The railroad reaches Reno, Nevada.

1869

The Central Pacific and Union Pacific meet at Promontory Summit.

LAST SPIKE
COMPLETING FIRST
TRANSCONTINENTAL
RAILROAD
DRIVEN AT THIS POINT
MAY 10TH 1869

To Find Out More

BOOKS AND JOURNALS

Ambrose, Stephen E. *Nothing Like It in the World: The Men Who Built the Transcontinental Railroad, 1863–1869.* New York: Simon & Schuster, 2000.

Blumberg, Rhoda. *Full Steam Ahead: The Race to Build a Transcontinental Railroad.* Hanover, PA: National Geographic Society, 1996.

Fraser, Mary Ann. *Ten Mile Day: And the Building of the Transcontinental Railroad.* New York: Henry Holt & Company, 1996.

ONLINE SITES

Building the Transcontinental Railroad
http://www.geocities.com/railstudents/building.html

Bureau of Land Management Environmental Education
Homepage: *http://www.CopyTK.com/*

Steel Rails and Iron Horses
http://www.blm.gov/education/railroads/trans.html

Central Pacific Railroad Photographic History Museum
http://cprr.org/Museum/index.html#Read

VIDEO

Modern Marvels: The Transcontinental Railroad. A&E Home Video, 1995.

Index

About the Author

Clark J. Evans was born in Altoona and raised in Duncansville, Pennsylvania. His father, John T. Evans, Sr., worked for the Pennsylvania Railroad at the Altoona repair shops. His grandfather James Hewitt and his great-grandfather Mark Sheldon Hewitt worked for the Pennsylvania Railroad as car inspectors at the Altoona Station. Mr. Evans earned his Eagle Scout award in 1963. While he was in the U.S. Air Force, he was in the fifty-two-flag honor guard for the White House and Pentagon from 1965 to 1967. He obtained an amateur radio license in 1974, call sign WA4DLL. Since 1981, Mr. Evans has written many books and articles on railroad history. He lives in Tampa, Florida, and has a son, Clark Jr.